CHRISTIAN POEMS & SONGS

I THAT FRIEND NAMED *Jesus!*

LILLIE MAE GRAVES

Copyright © 2022 by Lillie Graves

ISBN: 978-1-943342-47-1

All rights reserved. No part of this book may be reproduced, stored in a retrieval system, or transmitted in any form or by any means--electronic, mechanical, digital, photocopy, or any other---without prior permission from the publisher and author, except as provided by the United States of America copyright law.

That Friend Named Jesus
Christian Poems and Songs

Lillie Graves
novellg@sbcglobal.net

Destined To Publish
Flossmoor, Illinois
www.DestinedToPublish.com

Table of Contents

Poems

A Situation 2
All He Ask Is Just To Love 3
Believe Me It's True 4
Beware Of The Devil's Ways 5
Chips 7
Dear Lord 8
Don't Give Up 9
Fame. Look And Scene 10
God And You 11
God Cares 12
God Is Great 13
God's Power 14
God Will Be There 15
Happy Anniversary 17
How Nice It Is 18
I Want 19
It's Hard To Find 20
Keep Charge Of Me Lord 21
Lord Help Me To Love Them 23
My Enemies 25

My Little Child 26
Sitting On God's Hand 27
Stay With God. 28
That Friend Name Jesus 29
The Storms Of Life 31
Think It Over 32
To My Beloved Sister Frances 34
Today 35
What God Can Do 36
When You Have Done The Best You Can 37
Where Would You Be 38
Wouldn't It Be Nice. 39
Why It Took Me So Long 41
You May Never Awake Tomorrow 42

Songs

All And All 46
All He Ask For You To Do 48
All The Way 50
Be Patient 51
Christ Is The Answer 52
Day After Day 53
Don't Be Afraid To Trust Him 55
Don't Worry. 57
Don't You Think? 59

Go Pray	61
God Is Looking	62
God Will Be With You	63
God Won't Disappoint You, God Is Our Help	64
God Won't Let You Down	65
Ha Ha Hallelujah	66
Have You Done	67
He Did It All	69
He Never Fails You	70
He Never Leaves You	71
He Will Be There	74
He'll Be With You	75
He's Always On Time	77
He's The One	78
Heavenly Way	80
Help Me	81
Help Me (Love Them)	82
Help Me Lord	83
Help Me, Oh Lord	85
Hold On To Faith	86
How Much I Need You	87
I Am Yours Dear Lord	88
I Can't Make It Alone	89
I Don't Care	91
I Have Prayed	92

I Know Thee	93
I Love You	94
I Love You Lord	95
I Really Love You	97
I Understand	99
I Want To Be	100
I Will Live For You	101
I'll Stay With The Lord	102
I'm Not Worried	103
I'm So Glad	104
I'm Trying Lord	106
In My Father's Care	107
In The Valley	109
In This World	110
It'll Soon Be Over	112
Jesus Is All We Need	114
Jesus Is Leading Me	115
Jesus Is Mine	116
Jesus Is The Answer	117
Jesus Keep Me	118
Jesus Loves You	119
Jesus Paid It All	121
Jesus Will Stay With You	122
Just Believe	124

Just One Of Your Children	125
Just Trust In Me	126
Keep Me	127
Leave It With Jesus	128
Let Him Comfort You	129
Let It Be	130
Live For The Lord	131
Look	133
Love You	134
My Dear Tawanda	135
My Little Child	136
My Precious Lord	137
Oh Lord	138
Oh My Jesus	139
Prayer Our Father	140
Precious Lord	141
Put It In God's Hand	142
Really Need	143
Renew Me	144
Safely Through	146
See What God Has Done	147
Somewhere	149
Stand By The Lord	150
Sweetly Rest My Soul In Jesus	151

Take Faith 153
Take The Lord By His Hand 154
Thank You Lord 156
Thank You Lord For Giving Me A Son 157
The End Of The Tunnel 159
There's Nothing 160
Through This Day 161
Tomorrow 162
Travel This Christian Route 163
Wedding 165
Whatever It Takes Lord I Will Do 167
What He Can Do 170
What's Evers God's Wills 171
When It Seems No One Cares 172
Wherever We Are, Trust In God 174
Wherever You Are 175
Will Stand 177
Yes, Dear Lord 178

Poems

A Situation

You maybe in a
    dangerous situation,
But don't give up in hesitation
    Because God is near.

Things may look kinda
    dark at times,
But remember we are on God's mind
    and remember God is near.

Don't let old satan get
    you down,
When it seems no help is around
    because God is near.

Take faith as
    our shield,
And believe in God as we kneel
    because God is near.

He will protect and take
    care of us,
When in God we put our trust
    and for sure God will be near.

All He Ask Is Just To Love

When your loved one and some friends seems to have
    "No more to do with you"
And it's nothing you said or done in anyway
    "To cause them to treat you as they do"
But the only thing you've done is good and shown
    "Love to each and everyone"
But God suffered much more than that you see
    "For He gave His only begotten Son"
All He ask of us to do in times like these
    "Is pray to the Father up above"
Who have power to give us
    "That sweet, kind of tender love"
God knows the sorrow it brings to the heart
    "And He gives us love we should have for them too"
And supply us with love for them
    "That they should have for you"
That is really, really all one can
    "Pray, say or do"
For Christ died and shed His Blood on that Rugged cross
    "That we can have the Victory through
        All these things too"

Believe Me It's True

When you are sad, down and blue,
Remember God is there beside you,
    Believe me it's really true.

When the fiery darts are thick and fast,
God will take care of you while they pass.
    Believe me it's true.

When your burdens are too hard to carry,
God is there to help you to carry the cross you bare.
    Believe me it's true.

When you are in great distress,
God will help you through the stress.
    Believe me it's true.

When the devil comes like a storm,
God will not let you be harmed.
    Believe me it's true.

Beware Of The Devil's Ways

Beware of the devil and his conniving ways,
If you don't be careful he will get you unsaved.
For he is out doing his job very well,
Just getting poor souls and sending them to hell.

His spirit is here and everywhere,
Especially seeking those who is not careful and aware.
He's after those who are living for God,
Just waiting to touch them with his hot rod.

He will bring things very tempting to you,
But be aware of that scheme it's the devil's too.
The devil has nothing to gain or lose,
But we do for we have heaven or hell whatever we choose.

The devil likes to get people very confused,
But just forget it for that is one of his tools.
He loves to come in white sheet clothes,
For in that smooth way he gets many souls.

He's a terrible, terrible spirit,
And be very sure you can believe it.
Many, many people are going to hell everyday,
Because they chose the wide road instead of the narrow way.

It is so sad, so sad to see,
People pouring into hell for such a big fee.
Seems like people just choose hell for eternity, oh so bad,
Instead of heaven eternally, oh my how sad.

Chips

When the chips are down
    And things are rough,
Remember there's a God who
    Is really tough.
When things of life
    Look so dark,
Remember our Father is there
    Who is really tough
To carry our burdens
    That is too hard for us.

Dear Lord

You've seen the tears Dear Lord
    I've shed through the years
    As I live on earth down here

For you every day
I am not going back Dear Lord
Because I love you so
As onward I will go
To that home up above

You died for me Dear Lord
On that old rugged cross
So I wouldn't be lost
That is a very big cost

I thank you my Dear Lord
For saving my only soul
So I could have my eternal goal
    And be with you

Don't Give Up

Although our love one may not be saved,
Even though we have earnestly prayed,
That the Father above will continue to have mercy,
Upon these souls which is worth preserving.
As they live for the devil who is so rude,
And can give them nothing worth proving.
Some don't realize how dangerous it is,
To linger and wait on the devil's biz.
But God who in his tender loving care,
Is there to share the heavy burden we bare.
Sometimes it seems they would rather burn,
Than to give up to God and return.
But God all ways does his very best,
So all man kind can have sweet rest.
So don't give up in despair,
For God is there and really cares.
But God can't go over their will,
For He can only save those who yield.
So don't give up for there is God,
Who can only steer them with <u>love</u>, the <u>rod</u>.
But if they remain in sin and die,
Remember to say "God I tried and I tried,
And God I know you did your best,
That this soul would have peace and sweet rest.
And that's all we can really say or do,
For each person's <u>will</u> is the greatest <u>TOOL</u>.

Fame, Look And Scene

You don't have to have
    Fame or fortune
To help others to see you.
They'll see your life as you
    Live down here;
You don't have to have fame or fortune

You don't have to say, "Look at me
    I am saved, can't you see?"
They'll see your life and will tell you;
You don't have to say, "Look at me."

You don't have to make a scene
    To make others to notice you.
You can stay real calm and others will see;
You don't have to make a scene.

God And You

When something hard comes your way,
Just bow down and kneel and pray.
God is there right beside you
And believe it for it is true.
It may worry us quite a bit
But do remember God knows it.
The blessing will come right in time
And you will be doing just fine,
But don't forget to thank the Lord
For bringing you through this test that was so hard.

God Cares

When you are in a condition
That is hard to bear
Remember you have a
God who really cares

He is able to take care
Of whatever it maybe
No matter how impossible it may seem
Our God will take care of it, you see

The devil will come
In many, many ways
Trying very much to discourage you
But God is the one who has the last say

You can be very sure
God won't let you down
He has never lost a battle yet
And His word is very sound

God Is Great

Lord there are many things I want and desire,
    But help me to have faith in the darkest hour,
For Lord there is nothing impossible with you.
    If we pray and pray until we pray through,
You can give us the victory that can be ours,
    For God you got very great power,
Yes the devil will put up a great fight,
    But we don't have to worry for God's word is right.
You made our bodies that's so great,
    That helps me to have more faith.
Oh God you are so good to me,
    Thank you so much for hearing my plea.

God's Power

God is always there
When we need him.
Believe me it is true.
He'll never fail you.

God is always there
When everyone else is gone.
He may bring a verse, a prayer or a song
Just to help you as you go along.

Sometimes things may look so dark
But don't give up, keep going on.
God will be beside you
Believe me it is true.

At the end you will be a winner
Because God has power over all things;
Believe me it is true.
And God really, really loves you.

God Will Be There

In your most trying hour
And you seem to have no power
    God will be there.

When you don't know what to do
And you know no route to pursue
    God will be there.

You may see many faces
And go many places
    Yet God is there.

You may give up and go no further
But please remember my sister and brother
    God will be there.

You may toss and turn and cry
But by and by our tears will dry
    For God will be there.

You may be in great aggravation
But don't worry about the situation
    For God is there.

You may turn in bed at night
Of many situations that bring a fright
    Be calm God is there.

Sometimes there may be confusion
In something you are choosing
    But God will direct you there.

When you are in great temptations
Don't forget God's regulations
    For God will be there.

You may not get much in life down here
But over there is great so have no fear
    For God is there.

God hears and answers every prayer
And his spirit is everywhere
    You can be very sure God is there.

Happy Anniversary

Happy anniversary to a wonderful couple forever;
The one who God has put together.
May God bless you in this marriage,
With hearts full of love in your heart carriage.

May God bless you each day,
With a love that never goes away.
May God bless your love in a very safe way,
That no one can take it away.

May God bless you year after year,
With a marriage that's very secure.
May God bless you in crucial times,
That you will be protected by God the Father Divine.

May God bless you both together,
With a love that will last forever.
So have a Happy Anniversary,
For two nice people like you, you see.

How Nice It Is

How nice it is to have a sweet niece,
Who gave her life to God and will have sweet peace.

You have made the right choice in life,
But you will have the devil to fight.

You don't have the devil to fear,
For God will always be near.

To help you through those trials and tests,
And you will be alright if you stay in God's big nest.

The devil will come in different ways,
Just trying to get you as his slave.

Just keep on going for God my child,
For God is standing there with a big smile.

Christ died on the cross for everyone,
So at the end you could be forever with His Son.

I Want

I want to see my God in peace
I want to do His blessed will you see
I want to live to please my God
    Oh God I want to be with you

I want to live a Christian life
I want to do the things that's right
I want to live so others might see
    And turn and live for thee

I want to love my enemies and friends
I want to love those who hate me within
I want to love those that's prejudice
    And hope they see my Savior's face

It's Hard To Find

It's hard to find someone
Who cares, cares for you in this day and time.
It's hard to find someone who
Will get under the burden and pray for you in this day and time.
It's hard to find someone
Who will talk, talk to you in this day and time.
It's hard to find someone who
Loves you, loves you in this day and time.
It's hard to find someone who will
Stand by you, stand by you in this day in time.
It's hard to find someone who
Will be a friend, be a friend to you in this day and time.
I've found the one who cares
For your needs and help in this day and time.
It's God, the Father, who
Gave His Son, Jesus Christ, to die for you and me.
So Jesus Christ died on the cross
For you and me, you and me,
So we can have life eternally.

Keep Charge Of Me Lord

When we awake in the morning anew,
And there are many things to do,
It is good to kneel and pray,
"Take complete charge of me Lord today."

As we go about our daily chores,
And the devil make it seems such a bore,
Keep on toiling in the same way,
And say "take complete charge of me Lord today."

The trials and test that come before the day end,
We can really live free from sin,
If we only will think and pray,
"Lord take charge of me this day."

When deep persecution comes our way,
The best thing to do is kneel and pray,
To the Heavenly Father above,
And say "Lord, please keep me secure in Thy sweet love."

When things look so dark, weary and dreary,
Our Heavenly Father just says "Oh, don't get weary".
"Did you hear my soft voice say,
I will keep charge of you today"?

When temptation comes buzzing by,

Just turn your head and look at the sky,
And say "my God will keep me in the right way",
By praying "Lord, my Lord, keep charge of me today".

When times are hard and money is short,
We can depend on God to do His part,
By praying "Father, supply my needs this day",
And He will take charge and answer in the same way.

When the work is done and the day is over,
It's real good to look at the devil over your shoulder,
And say "I am, yes I am still in the right way,
For my God, yes my God kept control of me today".

Thank you Father for being so kind,
And taking charge of my mind.
Thank you Father very much too,
For keeping charge of my heart and body as you usually do.

Thank you for keeping charge of all of me,
So that I may be in glory with Thee.
Thank you for keeping charge of my soul,
For it is "Yours" only to have and to hold.

Lord Help Me To Love Them

Lord there are many people who
Make me sad,
And many who
Treat me bad,
But Lord help me to love
Them the same.

Lord there are those who
Tell lies on me
And falsely accused me you see,
But Lord help me to love
Them the same.

Lord there are those who
Hate me because of the color of my face
And of my race,
But Lord help me to love
Them the same.

Lord there are those who
Judge me in this Christian race
And grin in my face,
But Lord help me to love
Them the same.

Lord there are those who
I have helped in different ways,
And now that they are doing well, they have not much to say,
But Lord help me to love
Them the same.

Lord there are those who
Steal from me
And will keep it you see,
But Lord help me to love
Them the same.

Lord there are those who
Talk mean and say ugly words to me,
And they mean it you see,
But Lord help me to love
Them the same.

My Enemies

Oh, my enemies are coming against me
In the way in which they are.
They are jealous and I know it
But God got the power to stop them
For there's nothing impossible with God.

I want to love them.
That's what God wants me to do
So Lord help me all the way through.
Help me to love them for love is beautiful
And maybe they will live for you.

I will pray for them because they really need it
And I will know God will talk to their hearts.
Their souls are in danger.
Oh, how sad it would be for them
To be in eternity forever burning
Without ceasing eternally.

My Little Child

Are you down, unhappy and blue?
    You know something God still loves you.
You may have cried and cried all night,
    With God by our side everything will be alright.

Things down here is full of many disappointing things,
    But God is still there just give him a ring,
And He's right there with a listening ear,
    And He's been there down through the years.

You may have problems, oh those awful problems,
    But you know our Father can solve them.
For there is nothing impossible with God,
    And He will stop the devil with his guiding rod.

God loves you my little child,
    And He is right there standing with a beautiful smile,
Saying, "Trust me through those awful trials and tests
    And I will give you that needed sweet rest."

Sitting On God's Hand

Over the hill you can not see,
Down in the valley you may be,
But there is someone you can count on indeed,
It's Jesus Christ sitting on God's right hand.

There are the mountains so high in the sky,
And they look too high for you and I,
But there is someone right by our side,
Remember it's Jesus sitting on God's right hand.

Over the seas my Father will be,
He never forgets you and me.
He's right beside you, you can believe,
It's Jesus Christ sitting on God's right hand.

On the land He's right there at hand,
He's right there as close as He can.
So stay close beside Him right in His plan,
It's worth it to be with Him up above seeing Him sit on God's right hand.

Stay With God

Lord I want to stay with You each day,
So I can be with you in the Heavenly way.
I have to pray very, very hard,
Just to be with my Savior and Lord.

The devil will come in many, many ways,
Just to try and get you unsaved.
But through much prayer and fasting too,
You can keep saved and keep the Master with you.

For God got more power than the devil ever had,
So we don't have to worry but be very glad.
For we can be assure that our Father has gone to prepare,
A very, very beautiful mansion for us to be with Him forever there.

That Friend Name Jesus

When things in life get pretty rough,
And everything seems so tough,
Remember you have a friend name
    Jesus.

When your burdens are hard to bear,
And it seems no one cares,
Remember you have a friend name
    Jesus.

When your loved ones fail you too,
And you don't know what to do,
Remember you have a friend name
    Jesus.

When your loved one pays you no mind,
And worse than that, they aren't even kind,
Remember you have a friend name
    Jesus.

When you are there all alone,
And everyone else is gone,
Remember you have a friend name
    Jesus.

When trials and tests come your way,

And it seems they are there to stay,
Remember you have a friend name
    Jesus.

When your work is finished down here,
You really don't have to fear,
Because you are going home to be with that friend name
    Jesus.

The Storms Of Life

When the storms of life
    Make you sad and blue,
Just kneel down on your knees
And pray and God will work all things
    Out for you.

Just tell the devil to get behind you
    And he will surely flee.
God got more power than
    The devil you see.

God has never lost a battle you know
    And that is really true.
All the way to Heaven, He
    Will stand by you.

Think It Over

Yea as you walk with the devil in sin down here.
You really do have to fear.
It is really dangerous out there.
We don't know how much time we have to spare.
    So think it over

In sin he leadeth you a little at a time,
And that way we don't know it's with our mind.
He preparest before you a good time life,
And you will think my what a wonderful sight.
    So think it over

You will go right to sin strong,
And you will be doing all kinds of wrongs,
And after that you will soon fit in,
With all of that filth of sin.
    So think it over

If you don't change, when Jesus plead,
He will not put his self on you, He will just leave.
If God give you another chance take it,
For He may not come again to deal with your soul and that's it.
    So think it over

Many things happen between God and man.
You are the only one who knows his command.

When you go through the valley of the shadows of death,
God won't be there to comfort you and that is that.
But the devil will be there,
To put you in the lake of fire and the pain you will have to bear.
    So think it over

It's so sad to go in eternity unprepared,
When you could have eternal life and God will be there.
Which road you choose is your choice.
Satan will be there with his ugly voice.
    So think it over

The devil will have conquered his goal,
For he will have won your soul,
To be with him burning in eternity,
Forever and ever eternally.
    So think it over

God will be unhappy too,
For He has done His best for you,
So you could have been with Him up above,
Where there is peace, joy, happiness and love.
    So think it over

To My Beloved Sister Frances

Frances you are a beautiful person
You love everyone including your enemies
You help the poor in the way they need it
You get under the burden for all problems
for others and pray also
Even though you don't feel good you still help others
You are not high minded
You will do other work that is not in your profession
for an income
You will stand by a person until their need is done
You have your hard times, but you
make it through with God's
help
You are balanced in life
You have fed your enemies and kept them
You are friendly to people and treat them nice
even your enemies
Life has not been easy for you, but you are still going on
The most important thing of all, you are living for God,
and you will live again.

From your sister
Lillie

Today

How sad it is to see today,
People living any kind of way.

People committing all kind of sin,
That don't seem to bother them within.

Racial prejudice is an awful sin,
And people doing that will not in Heaven enter there in.

Adultery, fornication, envy, murder and strife,
Will cause you to miss eternal life.

Hatred, jealousy, malice and many more,
Will cause you to miss Heaven's shore.

It is sad, so sad to see,
People going to hell for such a big fee.

What God Can Do

When you done the best you can,
That is all God expects out of you,
For He knows how much you done and gone through.
For He realizes we're just a weak man
And He knows exactly just what to do.

When we've prayed and fasted too and we've cried also too,
Don't you think He can see and can hear,
For He heard every prayer and seen every tear,
For He got the power to work for you
And we really don't even have to fear.

For He had power to form the world
And He made the mountains that reach high in the sky
For He even made you and I and have power to calm the raging tide
And He can solve the deepest problem and calm swirls
We just have to keep our faith and not let it die.

We don't have to worry or even fret,
For God knew it was coming our way
All He really wants us to do is stay and pray
For He's never failed us, no not yet
And He only wants us to yield to his will day by day.

When You Have Done The Best You Can

When you have done the best you can do
And no more can be done,
Just pray to the Father above
And He will work all things out for you.

You may be in great distress
But don't go under the burden you bare,
For God is there with the help you need
And be very sure you'll be a success.

Life down here is very short
And it's up to us to make Heaven our goal
It will not be very easy
And it pays to keep going from the start.

There will be temptation, trials and tests that seem to have no end,
Only through God's help can we make it down here,
For in life, things get pretty rough,
But through God's power we can make it through thick and thin.

Where Would You Be

There is a lot of evil down here
    But without Jesus,
Where would you be?

There is stress in all ways of life
    But without Jesus,
Where would you be?

Yes, the old prejudice is coming back
    But with Jesus
We will be all right.

There is not much friendship this day and time
    But with Jesus
We will have a friend.

Oh, we can feel so lonely down here
    But without Jesus,
Where would you be?

The world is in a downward trend
    But with Jesus
We won't go down.

Wouldn't It Be Nice

Wouldn't it be nice if everyone love each other,
No matter what color the skin of another?

Wouldn't it be nice if no one have hatred in their hearts
And would love each other together and apart?

Wouldn't it be nice if one live free from sin
And would go to Heaven at the end?

Wouldn't it be nice if no one's heart had adultery, jealousy and strife
And be happy for each other in this life?

Wouldn't it be nice if no one was on alcohol and drugs of any kind
And would be enclosed in their right minds?

Wouldn't it be nice if everyone's heart was free from fornication and envy
And be thorough and cleansed within?

Wouldn't it be nice if our hearts were full with the fruits of the spirit
And have no fruits of the flesh in it?
Wouldn't it be nice if everyone would choose eternal life,
Than to leave this world without living right?

    Just wouldn't it be nice,
    To live right in this life.

Why It Took Me So Long

Lord I don't know why it took me so long
Just to seek for the heavenly Throne,
But I thank you for waiting so long
So I wouldn't miss my heavenly home.

Lord I love you so very, very much.
I want to keep with you in touch
So I can make it when things are so rough.
Oh my Lord I love you so much.

Lord I went so far astray,
And I did many things in those days.
Oh Lord I thank you for what you did say,
And I am glad that I did go and pray.

You May Never Awake Tomorrow

Dear People, I would like to say,
That the end of time is coming some day.
So don't forget our Christ who came,
To redeem all people in heaven we gain.

    So don't put off Salvation no farther,
    For you may never awake tomorrow.

The devil may offer many tempting things.
It's best to turn your back to his cutting rings,
Don't follow in his footsteps, it's a big mistake,
For your soul and eternal life is at stake.

    So don't put off salvation no farther,
    For you may never awake tomorrow.

So take God's word such good advice,
For you don't know whether He's coming day or night.
The devil will give you a big fight there,
But you don't know how much time you have to spare.

    So don't put off salvation no farther,
    For you may never awake tomorrow.

If God do not have complete possession of your soul,
Don't let the devil cheat you out of your goal.
For it's better to live in eternity,
Than to die and burn eternally.

    So don't put off salvation no further,
    For you may never awake tomorrow.

Songs

All And All

My all in all is in Jesus.
My all in all I gave to Him.
My burdens I have, I give Him them,
And the load is lighter to bare.

He works out all of your trials,
And He helps you through your test too.
You can count on Him, He tells the truth.
It's in the word, He never lies.

Oh Lord we love our children so much.
It hurts our heart to see them in sin,
And you are really their best friend.
Oh Lord, my God help them to see.

Oh Lord time is going so fast.
People don't seem to realize it.
The devil have blinded them quite a bit.
Oh Lord, my God have mercy on them.

We are working for You O Lord,
Helping the people to live for You.
You do Your best to save them too.
Oh help them to give their lives to You.

My all in all is in Jesus.
I am on my way to that home up above.
Where there will be joy, peace and love,
And I will see my Father's face.

My all and all is in Jesus.
Why not give Him your all and all too,
And let Him give His all to you,
So you will see His face in peace.

All He Ask For You To Do

All He ask for you to do
Is believe and be true
That is all He really expects out of you,
And He wants us to have faith
Even if we have to wait
All He ask us is believe
And we'll receive.

We may have many trials
But they are stepping stones my child,
To our home that's awaiting up above
Though we may be in them awhile
He wants us to have a smile
All He ask us is believe
And we'll receive.

All He ask us from the start
Is to love Him with all of our hearts,
And to never let our souls be destroyed
For it was Him who gave you life
When it seemed no hope was in sight,
All He ask us in return
Is not to burn.

You've may strayed so far away
And be in trouble and dismay
All He ask for you to do is kneel and pray,
For the devil is always there
To make you give up in despair
All He ask us is to yield
And you'll be filled.

CHORUS:

"All He ask us to do is to believe
And be true,
And live a life that is
Pleasing in His sight.
It's not hard you really see,
When we let "Jesus" the "Navigator" be
All He ask us is to do "our very best."

All The Way

[1]I want to follow Christ all of the way
[2]He will be leading us all the time
[3]If we follow in His footsteps
[4]We'll see our Father's face
[5]If we walk in our Father's footsteps all the way

[1]I want to walk with Christ everyday
[2]I want to be His child in every way
[3]He's been so good to me
[4]I want you to know
[5]I want to walk with Christ all of the way

CHORUS:

I want to be with Christ all of the time
I want to be with Christ all of the time
I am so happy I could be His child
I am going to follow Him all the way home

Be Patient

Be patient with Jesus,
He's been patient with you.
He never have left you,
So be patient my child,
He's working things out for you,
So be patient with Him,
For He's been patient with you all the way through.

There are so many things,
We want Him to do,
But sometimes we do,
Have to wait on Him.
He will answer your prayers,
Just as soon as He can,
So be patient with Him,
For He's been patient with you all the way through.

You don't have to worry,
Because his promises are true.
He never comes too late.
He is always on time.
You can be very sure,
He won't let you down,
So be patient with Him,
For He's been patient with you all the way through.

Christ Is The Answer

Christ is the answer to everything.
When in the valley, He is with you.
He never leaves you no not at all.
Christ is the answer to everything.

Christ is the answer when you are sick and in pain.
He never leaves you no not at all.
He will heal your body just only believe it.
Christ is the answer to everything.

Christ is the answer when darkness is around.
Keep your eyes on Jesus, He is right there.
Soon you will see the bright shining light.
Christ is the answer to everything.

Christ is the answer to eternal life.
Just kneel on your knees and ask for forgiveness.
He will forgive you and your sins will be gone.
Christ is the answer to everything.

Day After Day

There are trials and tests
That comes our way
At anytime
We never know, so

Sometimes we are sick
And in deep pain
That's hard to bare
And we do pray, so

You are there
When we are in sadness
To comfort our hearts
At that time, so

When we are in need
You do supply it,
We have to pray and
You will give it, so

CHORUS:

Day after day You are beside us,
Day after day You will guide us,
Day after day You've never failed us,
Day after day You takes care of us.

Don't Be Afraid To Trust Him

God will take care of everything.
    Don't be afraid to trust Him.
Whether things are bright or dim,
    Don't be afraid to trust Him.
He is there all of the time,
    Looking and watching over all that's thine.
He loves them each and everyone,
    So don't be afraid to trust Him.

When we are in much distress,
    He will be there and always bless
Whether others care or not,
    He's always there and cares a lots,
Keeping his word for He lie'th not ,
    For he's broken no promises not at all.
He will keep his word so firm and true,
    So don't be afraid to trust Him.

When the cares of life seem to get you down,
    Don't be afraid to trust Him.
He is always there standing around,
    Wanting very much to help you.
He never leaves you there,
    Without his love nor his care.
He's standing there with out stretched hands,
    Saying "Come on my child I'll help you."

When confusion comes your way,
    Just know it's the devil at his foul play.
He will even appear in white sheet clothes,
    Just another plot to fool you, you know
Just kneel and say a sweet prayer,
    To the Father above who is standing there.
He will show you where the devil is at work,
    So don't be afraid to believe God's word.

Don't Worry

We don't have to worry
In our Father's care
He is always there
To help us bear our cross

Things may come our way
As we live down here
We don't have to worry
In our Father's care

We don't have to worry
In our Father's care
You will know He's there
To help us through our trials

People may not treat us fair
Let God see you through
We don't have to worry
In our Father's care

We don't have to worry
In our Father's care
He is standing right there
To help us through life's care

The fiery darts are flying
In all kinds of ways
We don't have to worry
In our Father's care

We don't have to worry
In our Father's care
He sees us right there
Down under heavy stress

He is on His throne
And He cares for His own
We don't have to worry
In our Father's care

Don't You Think?

He gave His only life,
For you and for me.
He hung on the Rugged Cross,
Made of a tree.
Why not think about Jesus?
He loves you and me.
It's something He did for everyone.

He's done many things,
For you and for me.
Right here as we live,
On this earth down here.
You can see everyday,
What a mighty God we serve.
Don't you think about Jesus,
    Some of the time?

Oh, how thankful we should be,
To know a mighty God.
And see His Power,
And miracles too,
He has done down here for you and me.
Don't you think about Jesus,
    Some of the time?

CHORUS:

Don't you think about Jesus,
    Some of the time?
Don't you think about Jesus?
He is so kind.
He's been so good to you and me.
Don't you think about Jesus,
    Some of the time?

Go Pray

1. When your trial and test are heavy,
   When everyone seems to leave you,

2. When you're sick and down and out,
   When you are getting discouraged,

3. When the devil is getting you down,
   When you don't know what to do,

4. When you're confused and mixed up,
   When you're in great distress,

CHORUS:

Go pray to Jesus, Go pray to Jesus, Go pray to Jesus, Go pray to Jesus
And you will have sweet rest

God Is Looking

God is looking, looking
Down at you,
You can never, never
Hide from Him,
For He's seeing everything that you do,
So don't try to hide from Him.

God is listening, listening
To what you say,
So don't try to get away,
For He has heard whatever you did say,
So don't try to lie about it.

God knows, He knows
What's in your heart,
You can never, no never
Get away from Him,
For He knew it was there before you did,
So you never, no never get by Him.

God Will Be With You

Through the sunshine and the shadows
God will be with you all the time.
He will never forsake you,
God will be with you.

In the time of great depression
God will come and lift us out.
As we pray down on our knees
God will lift us out.

When we're in the stormy battle
With the devil all around,
God sees us in there fighting,
God will rescue us.

When it seems no one cares
Just believe our Father does.
He's right there beside us,
God is always there.

God Won't Disappoint You, God Is Our Help

God is our help in trouble
When no one will be
Take His word and believe
God is our help indeed

Don't cry my little one
Just keep your eyes on God
Your problem will be none
If you will believe in His Son

God will help you to love them
And be happy too
He will be right there with you
Oh God will not disappoint you

God will not disappoint you
God will not disappoint you
He will work out all things for you
Oh God will not disappoint you

God Won't Let You Down

God will never, no never let you down;
He's always there standing around.
He will always take care of His child,
So be at peace, be at peace with my God.

God will help you with your problems my child,
So don't give up my child in the trial;
For He will always stand by your side.
So be at peace, be at peace with my God.

God will not forsake, forsake you my child;
He will be there in the darkest hour.
He will be there when no one else is,
So be at peace, be at peace with God.

Ha Ha Hallelujah

HA HA HALLELUJAH HA HA HALLELUJAH
HA HA HALLELUJAH
WE LOVE OUR LORD

HA HA HALLELUJAH HA HA HALLELUJAH
HA HA HALLELUJAH
HE LOVES US TOO

HA HA HALLELUJAH HA HA HALLELUJAH
HA HA HALLELUJAH
WE'LL SERVE OUR LORD

HA HA HALLELUJAH HA HA HALLELUJAH
HA HA HALLELUJAH
WE'LL KEEP HIS WORD

HA HA HALLELUJAH HA HA HALLELUJAH
HA HA HALLELUJAH
WE'RE REACHING OUR GOAL

HA HA HALLELUJAH HA HA HALLELUJAH
HA HA HALLELUJAH
FOR OUR DEAR SOUL

Have You Done

Have you prayed for the sick
In the hospital and the home?
Did you stay by their side
Until they needed you no more?
Have you done what you could?

Have you helped those that's poor
Or in temporary financial need
Until they could make it on their own
And they didn't need you anymore?
Have you done what you could?

Have you saw some unhappy faces?
Did you try to cheer them up
With a kind and smiling face
That would come from your heart?
Have you done what you could?

Have you stood by the side
Of someone in deep grief?
Did you pray for them
While standing by their side?
Have you done what you could?

Have you helped the ones that's blinded
By showing them all the kindness?
Did you help the disabled
In anyway you could help them?
Have you done what you could?

Have you lived a Christian life
That is pleasing in God's eyesight?
Have you been trying to please God
And not to please man?
Have you done what you could?

Have you helped some poor souls
To see where they needed to change
And live for God the rest of their life
And make Heaven their eternal home?
Have you done what you could?

CHORUS:

Have you done what you could?
Have you done what you could?
For my Jesus is so good,
And He loves everyone,
Have you done what you could?
For He gave His only life,
So we could have eternal life.
Have you done what you could?
Have you done what you could?

He Did It All

He gave His Son Jesus Christ,
Who died upon the cross,
That we may live for Him down here,
And we don't have man to fear.

He gives us love for all mankind.
He gives us grace for our test and trials.
He gives us help for the pain we bare,
And you can believe God really cares.

When the cares of life gets you down,
He'll be there to help you out,
For He know what's in the future you see,
So don't worry He'll take care of thee.

CHORUS:

He did it all my Jesus
He did it all for you
He did it all you see
He did it all for you and me

He Never Fails You

He'll never fail you, he'll never fail you.
If danger is all, all around you,
He will protect you, He will protect you,
From all harm, that, ever bewale's you.
He'll never fail you, he'll never fail you.
No matter what the danger will be.

He never fails you, no matter what ails you.
He is right there, there beside you.
He surely will help you, yes surely will help you
From everything that is ailing you.
He never will fail you, He never will fail you
No matter what the case will be.

When you're in trouble, he'll never fail you.
His hands are right there, Ready to help you
Just hold on to them, he'll lift you right out
Of all your troubles that was so rough
He wouldn't fail you, He wouldn't fail you
For He's promised you help in His word.

When others fail you He'll never fail you.
He's up above supplying us with love
For those who have failed us, and caused many tears,
That we've been shedding, down through the years.
He'll give you a prayer, to help us out.
He's the best friend that you can ever have.

He Never Leaves You

Though your problems be great or small
He is able to solve them all
    He never leaves you
    He never leaves you
It may seem impossible to you, you see
Just take it to Him and let it be
    He'll never fail you
    He'll never fail you
Sometimes we prayed so very long
Until it seem our faith is gone
    He never left thee
    He never left thee

When your finances is growing short
He knew that right before the start
    He never leaves you
    He never leaves you
He will come right now and help you out
If we believe and never doubt
    He never leaves you
    He never leaves you
For in His word He has promise you
Our food and shelter and clothing too
    He never leaves you
    He never leaves you

When the devil presses you on every side
Yield not to discouragement under the tide
    He haven't left thee
    He haven't left thee
Just trust in God like Job did too
And see He bring you right on through
    He never left thee
    He never left thee
He hears your prayer with a listening ear
And there's no reason to have a fear
    He never leaves you
    He never leaves you

When you are sick & down & out
He stops the pain that it brings about
    He never leaves you
    He never leaves you
For He know just that you're going through
For He been through the pain and death too
    He never leaves you
    No never leave you
For He hung on the rugged cross, the tree,
And said by stripes you're healed you see
    He never leaves you
    He never leaves you

Though death may leave an awful blow
But Jesus see and really know
    He never leaves thee

He never leaves thee
For He conquered death, hell and the grave
So that our love one might be saved
　　　He'll never leave them
　　　He'll never leave them
Especially if they've lived for God down here
They will reign with Him through all the years
　　　He never left them
　　　He never left them

CHORUS:

He never leaves you standing there
He is there with His loves and care
　　　He never leaves you
　　　He never leaves you
He is always standing there
With His great love, mercy, and care
　　　He never leaves you
　　　He never leaves you

He Will Be There

There will be sunshine and the rain,
Living for God it's the same.
There'll be good days and the bad,
And some days that is sad.
God can help you through them all.
He'll never let you fall.
He will be there, He will be there to rescue you.

There will be burdens hard to bare,
Let God have them He really cares.
He'll take care of each one.
Just pray to God's only Son,
He'll be there all the time.
He'll work them out just fine.
He will be there, He will be there to rescue you.

There will be temptations of all kinds,
Leave them to God He never minds.
You will overcome every one,
By the help of God's only Son,
Over the temptations that faced you,
You've won the victory too.
He will be there, He will be there to rescue you.

He'll Be With You

Many times it may seem,
That the Savior isn't there,
But He is, so don't give up in despair.
He is right by your side.
You may not know.
He is there all of the time.

The devil may be all around.
You will know he is there,
Because confusion will be all around.
You just have to kneel and pray,
For it to go away.
He'll be with you all of the time.

Through the darkness of the night,
Keep your eyes on Jesus Christ,
Because God is there with the light.
He will not let you down.
He is never too late.
He'll be with you all of the time.

CHORUS:

He'll be with you through it all.
He won't forsake you, not at all.
He will always be there,
Because He really cares.
He'll be with you through it all.

He's Always On Time

God's never too late, He's always on time.
    He's always on time, He's always on time.
He sees what we need before we do.
    He's always on time, He's always on time.
He never forgets us, you can be very sure.
    He's always on time, He's always on time.
        God is always on time.

He's always there before we know.
    He's always on time, He's always on time.
He'll never, no never, let you down.
    He's always on time, He's always on time.
When we trust in God, we can be very sure,
    He's always on time, He's always on time.
        God is always on time.

There is nothing impossible with the Lord.
    He's always on time, He's always on time.
Just have faith in God up above.
    He's always on time, He's always on time.
He will answer your prayers you've sent up there.
    He's always on time, He's always on time.
        God is always on time.

He's The One

When God's arms are all around you,
You can feel so safely,
It's the kind and sweetest feeling you can have.
He's the one whose love don't change.
He's the one who never fail you.
He's the one that you can trust in all the time.

Every day that we live,
He always watches over us,
Like the Shepherd that cares over the sheep.
He's the one who protect us.
He's the one who never forsakes us.
He's the one who you can count on all the time.

The earth was created by Him.
Man was made by His hands.
By His breath we became a living soul.
He's the one who have all power.
He's the one we should follow.
He's the one we're going to be with in eternity.

CHORUS:

He's the one who really loves you.
He's the one who stands beside you.
He's the one who never lies.
He's the one, He's the one.
He's the one who won't forget you.
He's the one who never leaves you.
He's the one who really cares about you.

Heavenly Way

God's the best friend I have
I know it for it's deep within
He'll stand beside until the end
He's the best friend you can have

He has done many things for me
And that's really really the truth
He never never let me down
He was right there all around

Oh how I love my Father up above
He's gone to prepare a beautiful home
For all of His children everywhere
And we will always forever roam.

CHORUS:

I will walk in the heavenly way
That's the way God wants me too
He's so loving, kind, patient and good
I'm going to walk in the heavenly way

Help Me

Help me Jesus through this day,
To stay in the Heavenly way.
Give me grace to go through this trial,
So I can make it every step of the mile.
I love you so very much,
So help me to stay in touch.

Help me Jesus in times like these,
To keep praying down on my knees.
Without you I couldn't do anything,
For I am just a helpless human being.
Help me to carry the cross to bear,
For it's no more than fair.

Help me Jesus to love everyone,
Because of the death of Your Son,
That's the greatest thing You could do for us,
And I appreciate it very much.
How nice it will be if others could see,
How good it is to belong to Thee.

Help Me (Love Them)

Help me to love those that do me wrong
Help me to show them plenty of love
Help them to see Christ in my life
Help them to see God in Heaven above
Help them to give their heart to you

Help me to show plenty of kindness
To every one that I see each day
Help me to have a smile on my face
And to help cheer someone that is down on my way
Help me to please You all the way home

Help me to show to show everyone on my journey
That I love them very much
Help me to tell every one about You
So they won't get in the devil's clutch
So they can be with you up above.

Help Me Lord

Help me Lord to live today,
The way it pleases You I pray.
Help me Lord that I may show my friends,
When we live for You, we're sure to win
No matter what the problems may be
Through the darkest moment we may see
That our power is unlimited and strong,
When our souls to You belong.

Help me Lord that I may stay
In this straight and narrow way,
For heaven is cheap at any cost
Than to lose our souls and be lost.
Help me Lord that I may see,
When my brothers and sisters are in need,
For it is more blessed to give
Than receive, as in this life we live.

Help me God to live this Christian life
Free from jealous, murder, envy and strife.
There are many, many more sins too
That I surely don't want to commit or do,
So through my life that others may see
And turn and live forever with thee
And have peace, joy, hope and love,
So they can be with You above.

Help me Lord to have a never failing love for You
And all my love ones, friends and enemies too,
Even for those to hate me because of my race
That they too might see Your Heavenly face,
For those who do me wrong intentionally
Help them Lord to even see Thee.
It might be kind of hard you see
But it's worth it all to be forever with Thee.

Oh, sometimes it seems things be so dark
But keep me safe as You did those in Noah's Ark,
For the sun will shine after a while,
If we trust in God through the devil's wilds,
For He loves us and will never let you down,
When we stand strong upon God's solid grounds,
And hear and answers every prayer we pray,
As we pray His will be done day by day.

Help Me, Oh Lord

Help me, oh Lord this trial is so hard.
Help me to be as You, you see.
Help me this time to be as Thine.
Take my hand and hold it as a band,
So I can make it through.

I'm just Your little child, I need You right now.
You helped me so much, please keep me in touch,
For You got all power, You are not a coward,
So come and help me through this trial.

You never let me down, You are always around,
Listening to our prayers that we are sending up there,
That we can have peace if only we can reach,
And we could trust, if we have our Savior's cup.

CHORUS:

Help me, oh Lord, Help me, oh Lord,
Help me, oh Lord for down here it's hard.
I can't make it without You, I know
You can do it so stand by
My side in this trial.

Hold On To Faith

When you're in trials and tests
Just hold on to faith
It will carry you through
So just hold on to faith

When temptation comes your way
Just hold on to faith
It will carry you through
So just hold on to faith

When the devil comes against you
Just hold on to faith
It will carry you through
So just hold on to faith

When sickness comes your way
Just hold on to faith
It will carry you through
So just hold on to faith

CHORUS:

Just hold on to faith
Just hold on to faith
That's the best thing to do
Just hold on to faith

How Much I Need You

Lord you see how much
    I need you
Lord you see how much
    I need you
    I cannot make it without you
Lord you see how much
    I need you

Though I am sick in my body
And it looks dark and cloudy
But with God's help I'll make it through
Lord, you see I really need you

On the stormy sea of life
Keep my faith strong as I fight
The devil that is all around me
Lord you see I really need you

Give me strength for this day
And give me strength all of the way
As I go through life down here
Oh Lord, you see I need you

Jesus, my Savior, hold to my hand

I Am Yours Dear Lord

I am Yours dear Lord
Because You died for me
I love You my Lord
Because You set me free
You took my place dear Lord
Upon the rugged cross
All of my days my Lord
I will live for You

I have faith my Lord
Because Your word is true
I have seen my Lord
What You can really do
There is really nothing
Impossible with You
All of my days my Lord
I will live for You

All of my days my Lord
I will live for You
That is what my Lord
I really want to do
I'm not afraid of man
As I live down here
All of my days my Lord
I will live for You

I Can't Make It Alone

God sees the devil all of the time
So don't fear when the devil is near
God is right by my side at all times
Without God I couldn't make it alone

I am very dependent upon God
For everything that I need
He sees the future I cannot see
Without God I couldn't make it alone

When trials and tests are very hard
God is right there to see me through
He never leaves me alone
Without God I can't make it alone

When I am sick and in pain He is there
To take away the pain I bare
God loves me and He really cares
Without God I couldn't make it alone

CHORUS:

I cannot make it alone
I cannot make it alone
I need my Father's help
To carry the load
I cannot make it alone
Ohh---o---o I cannot make it alone

I Don't Care

I don't care whether people love me.
I don't care for God is with me.
I don't care what people say about me.
I just want to please Christ you see.

I don't care if people do scorn me,
For they did more to Christ you see.
I don't care what people think of me.
I just want to be as Christ you see.

I don't care the color of my skin,
For God made me and He's pleased within.
I don't care about having a friend,
For God's my friend and He'll be until the end.

I Have Prayed

I have prayed many a prayer,
Sometimes in great despair,
But my Jesus was standing right there,
And He looked at me and smiled
Saying, "Don't give up my child,
For I am standing,
Yes standing by your side."

So keep on praying my child,
God will answer you in a while,
And I'll be with you every step of the mile.
I will never let you down;
Keep standing on God's solid ground,
For He will never, no
Will never let you down.

CHORUS:

Yes He is standing,
Yes standing by your side.
Saying don't give up in the tide,
For it's not worth it, not
Worth it my sweet child.

I Know Thee

I am glad I know Thee.
You're the best friend I have had.
I know You love me.
I can see it so plainly,
Oh, Oh, Oh Lord I love You.

I don't want to doubt You,
Things are here at Your command.
I know it is true.
You have done a lot for me.
Oh, Oh my Lord I love You.

We can really trust You.
You've never failed me yet.
You've kept Your word,
And that's enough for me.
Oh, Oh my Lord I love You.

I Love You

1. I love You (I love You) my Lord (my Lord).
   You've carried me (You've carried me) this far (this far).

2. I want You (I want You) to stay with me (to stay with me).
   And I'll be happy (And I'll be happy) to stay with Thee (to stay with Thee).

3. There are many (are many) who don't care (don't care).
   They keep on wondering (keep wondering) unprepared (unprepared).

4. Death may come (may come) any time (any time).
   God is merciful (He's merciful) and so kind (so kind).

CHORUS:

My Lord is coming (oh yes) He's coming
(Oh yes) To take me home (oh yes)
To take me home (oh yes) where
I will never (no never) roam down
Here (roam down here) I will be with Him, (oh yes)
All the time (all the time)

I Love You Lord

I thank You Lord, I thank You Lord
For saving my soul
I want to very much make Heaven my goal
So I could not go to a burning hell
I thank You Lord, I thank You Lord
For saving my soul

I love You Lord, I love You Lord
And I know You love me
You've been by my side at all times I see
You've never failed me, no not at all
I love You Lord, I love You Lord
Because You love me

You've been my guide, You've been my guide
And You've been my light too
I've made it this far because of You
You give me all I need at all times
You've been my guide, You've been my guide
Oh I love You

You've helped me, You've helped me
To hold on to You
I want to be one of those chosen few
So I can be with You eternally
Please help me, please help me
To stay on with You

I Really Love You

Oh yes, I really love You Lord.
Oh yes, I really love You Lord.
You've been so good to me my Lord.
You've never turned anyone away.
You're there when others are gone away.
My Lord I love You so.

I want to be as Thee my Lord.
I want to be as Thee my Lord.
Your life is so beautiful.
I love it in my heart, You see.
I want to be as You, You see.
So I can be with Thee.

I want to please You, my Lord.
I want to please You, my Lord,
At all times so that others can see,
And turn and live for You, You see.
They will be happy in their soul,
And they will have eternal life.

When you are depressed my child.
When you are depressed my child.
Just kneel on your knees and pray.
He will hear your faintest prayer.
You can be sure He'll answer them.
So just have faith in God.

God can solve all problems in life.
God can solve all problems in life.
Just put your trust in God's hands.
Just believe it because He really can.
So don't let the devil get you down.
God will never fail you.

I Understand

I understand it now
I understand it now
I understand it now
I understand salvation now

There was a time
I did not understand
What it was all about
But now I understand

There was some time
I was quite confused
About many things
But now I understand

I thank God for helping
Me to understand
It is very clear
I understand it now

We go through our trials
We go through our test
Sometimes we may not get our rest
But one day it will soon be all over

I Want To Be

I want to be
With my God you see
He's done a lot for me
He'll never fail you
He never will leave you
He'll never forsake you
He'll always be there
Whenever you need Him

He will answer your Prayers
That we send up there
To help us to bare
The problems we face
With His love and Grace
We'll make it through them all
No matter how hard
You can count on God

When we're feeling weak
Just kneel down and seek
Please do not retreat
For God is right there
To give you the strength
That you really need
Through the dark valley
He will be there with you

I Will Live For You

I am yours dear Lord
Because you died for me
I love you my Lord
Because you set me free
You took my place my dear Lord
Up on the rugged cross
All of my days my Lord
I will live for you

I have faith my Lord
Because your word is true
I have seen my Lord
What you can really do
There is really nothing
Impossible with you
All of my days my Lord
I will live for you

All of my days my Lord
I will live for you
That is what my Lord
I really want to do
I'm not afraid of man
As I live down here
All of my days my Lord
I will live for you

I'll Stay With The Lord

When we're with the Lord
We don't have to worry
Our burdens we carry
He will carry them for you

When people do you wrong
He sees that too
And He always knows what to do
You can see again His power is great

He will give you the love
We need down here
For our enemies that are so near
So I'll trust in God without any fear

CHORUS:

I'll stay with the Lord
He is my best friend
He'll stay with me until the end

I'm Not Worried

Things in life can make you worry
As you live on Earth down here
But my Father, He knows the future you see
So I'm not worried anymore

The devil will come in many ways
To make you worry in life down here
But my Father sees the devil, you see
So I'm not worried anymore

CHORUS:

I'm not worried anymore
I'm not worried anymore
Because my Father is over the whole universe
So I'm not worried anymore

I'm So Glad

I'm so glad that
Jesus saved my soul
Jesus saved my soul
Jesus saved my soul
Oh, I'm so glad I'm
under His control
under His control
under His control
Oh, I'm so glad I'm
under His control
under His control to stay

I'm so glad there's
room for everyone
room for everyone
room for everyone
I'm so glad He
sacrificed His Son
sacrificed His Son
sacrificed His Son
Oh, I'm so glad He
sacrificed His Son
sacrificed His Son for me

I'm so glad that
Jesus made me whole
Jesus made me whole
Jesus made me whole
I'm so glad I'm
ready to go
ready to go
ready to go
Oh, I'm so glad I'm
ready to go
ready to go home

I'm Trying Lord

I'm trying Lord to live right down here
And I need You to be very near
I can't make it by myself You see
Oh Lord help me to stay with Thee

The devil will come and be all around
Help me Lord to stay very sound
He will be there and try to get my soul
Oh Lord help me not to lose my goal

The devil comes in many, many ways
Help me Lord not to ever stray
Keep my eyes on You up above
And stay secure in Your wonderful love

Help me Lord to stay humble at Your feet
And keep praying there to be very sweet
Help me to be very loving too
And stay there always with You

In My Father's Care

I am in my Father's care
Everyday everywhere.
He will never let you down.
He is always around.
Yes, He loves you all the time,
When others leave you behind,
Oh, I'm so happy I am in my Father's care.

When I'm in my Father's care,
He is with me in there.
He will always be with you
And carry you through.
All test and trials you may meet,
He'll be there to defeat.
Oh, I'm so happy I am in my Father's care.

I love being in my Father's care.
He treats people good and fair.
He's so good and treats you nice,
And He treats everyone right.
Oh, what a wonderful Father we serve,
Even to those who don't deserve.
Oh, I'm so happy I am in my Father's care.

CHORUS:

I am in my Father's care
And I am so happy that I am there.
He has always been good to me,
When He speaks the devil has to flee,
And I am so happy I am in the Father's care.

In The Valley

Down in the valley
You may be,
But God is seeing you and me.
He will help you at all times,
And you'll know He's there.
He'll be there with you and me.

He knows that valley,
Because He is there.
He's been there many years, and He always cares.
He's wiped away many, many tears.
He's done this many, many times,
For I have been a witness for many years.

Out of the valley
You will come,
For in every case He's always won.
You'll be very happy,
For what He has done,
So give others this good advice.

In This World

Oh Lord I want to be,
As You want me You see,
In this world, oh in this world.

The devil may try to defeat me,
As I seek for Thee,
In this world, yes in this world.

Oh Lord I love You so.
I want to be ready to go,
In this world, yes in this world.

I want to keep in touch,
With You very much,
In this world Lord, in this world.

I want to love everyone,
And see Christ, His Son,
In this world, yes in this world.

We don't have to fear,
Because He is near,
In this world Lord, in this world.

When He comes for me,
I want to be ready you see,
In this world Lord, in this world.

I want to live right, here,
In God's eye sight near,
In this world, yes in this world.

CHORUS:

Lord I want to live right in this world,
    Down here, Down here.
There are many temptations that will come your way.
Lord I want to live right in this world.

It'll Soon Be Over

It'll soon be all over on earth down here.
You can see it so plainly and know it's near.
There are so many things that make it so clear.
So stay ready, so you will know,
Whenever He comes you'll be ready to go.

There're so many people that carelessly wait.
They don't seem to realize their soul is at stake.
They keep on wondering in sin till too late.
Then they are soon gone to hell you see,
And that is a sad place forever to be.

It'll soon be all over, you can still be His child
All you have to do is repent as you bow.
God will hear your prayer and forgive you right now.
You'll never regret it, it's the best thing to do,
And God will be happy with what you did choose.

There will be trials and tests that you will meet.
God will be there forever for you to seek.
And you can be very sure that He's there for keeps,
God never lies so just believe,
Our souls are important and always will be.

It'll all be all over for everyone.
God gave us Jesus His precious Son.
He gave us His life and the victory He won.
He did it for you and did it for me,
So we could go to Heaven and forever be.

Jesus Is All We Need

When we are in need He supplies
Us with whatever we need
Just have faith in my Father
He won't let you down
Jesus is all we need

People will turn you down
When you need them so very much
They may leave you and fail you
But God will be with you
Jesus is all we need

He's done so much for me
He will do the same for you
When we have our problems
My Father will solve them
Jesus is all we need

CHORUS:

Jesus is all we need
Jesus is all we need
He comes to our rescue
All of the time
My Jesus is all we need

Jesus Is Leading Me

He's never failed me not at all.
He takes care of me in every way.
Just lean on the Savior, He won't let you fall.
He'll be with you all the way home.

What a mighty God we are serving down here.
His power is unlimited and very strong,
So don't fear the devil he can't get by God,
Just remember His power all the way home.

Just work for God while living down here,
What work He gives you do it very well.
Don't let the devil hinder you no not at all.
Be faithful and work all the way home.

CHORUS:

All the way home my Jesus is leading me.
All the way home never more to roam.
Jesus is leading me each step of the way.
Jesus is leading me all the way home.

Jesus Is Mine

Jesus is mine all of the time
He's never failed me, not at all
He's always with me in the darkest hour
Jesus is mine all of the time

He's always there when others are gone
To comfort my heart when I'm alone
He whispers sweet peace to my listening ear
Jesus is mine all of the time

Jesus Is The Answer

Jesus is the answer
    When we are in trial and test.
Jesus is the answer
    When we are under stress.
Jesus is the answer
    When we are in restlessness.
Jesus is the One Who does His very best.

Jesus is the answer
    When we are down and out.
Jesus is the answer
    When the devil tosses you about.
Jesus is the answer
    When we are on the wrong route.
Jesus is the One Who will stay with you throughout.

Jesus is the answer
    When we don't know what to do.
Jesus is the answer
    Because He knows the route to pursue.
Jesus is the answer
    When He sees you fighting too.
Jesus is the One Who will carry you through.

Jesus Keep Me

JESUS KEEP ME ALL OF THE TIME
JESUS KEEP ME CLOSE TO THINE
JESUS HELP ME ALL OF THE WAY
AND KEEP ME CLOSE TO THINE

JESUS I CAN'T MAKE IT WITHOUT YOU
JESUS HELP ME WITH THIS TRIAL TOO
JESUS HELP ME ALL OF THE WAY
AND KEEP ME CLOSE TO THINE

JESUS HELP ME TO ALWAYS SEEK
YOU IN EVERTHING THAT I DO
JESUS HELP ME ALL OF THE WAY
AND KEEP ME CLOSE TO THINE

Jesus Loves You

Yes Jesus loves me,
Yes Jesus loves me,
Yes Jesus loves me,
For His word says so.

He's helped many people,
He's helped many people,
He's helped many people,
For myself I know.

He never leaves you,
He never leaves you,
He never leaves you,
For He loves you so.

Jesus will help you,
Jesus will help you,
Jesus will help you,
For He's promise to.

Jesus has mercy,
Jesus has mercy,
Jesus has mercy,
For He loves you so.

Why not follow Jesus,
Why not follow Jesus,
Why not follow Jesus,
To that home up above.

Jesus Paid It All

His cross was made of a tree,
Simon carried it you see.
They compelled him to do it
All the way, all the way to Calvary.

He was nailed to the cross you see
Through His hands and His feet,
They placed a crown of thorns upon
His head there at Calvary.

Blood was dripping from His body,
He was beaten with many stripes.
He said, "By them you are healed too."
For us at Calvary.

He thought God had forsaken Him,
He cried out with a loud voice,
"My God, My God why have You
Forsaken me?" That's what He did for you and me.

CHORUS:

Jesus paid it all for me,
Jesus paid It all for me.
He died and hung on the rugged cross.
My Jesus paid it all for me.

Jesus Will Stay With You

When you are seeking
For my dear Savior
He is right by your side

He never leaves you
He never fails you
He is there all the time

When you're in trials
When you're in tests
He is right there with you

He really knows
What you're going through
He will be there all of the time

The road may get rough
And things will get tough
He will see you safely through

Things may get dark
You may not see
Remember our Father is there with you

CHORUS:

Please stay with the Lord
He will never leave you alone
He has a love that will never fail
Jesus will stay with you

Just Believe

Just ask and believe and you shall receive,
    And what you are asking for,
    For God it is not too hard.
With God all things are possible,
    So don't give up my child,
For God will answer you in just a little while.

He will never let you down, He is always around.
    He sees your every need,
    Just bow down on your knees,
And ask the Father above,
    And you'll receive His love.
You can count on His word and count on His love.

Just One Of Your Children

Lord, I try and try again
I want You to be my friend
As my friend, I'm sure to win
Lord, I want to make it in.

When I'm down, please lift me up
From the things that are so tough
Give me grace for each one
Oh Lord, I want to see Your Son.

I have cried so many tears
Over all of these years
Lord, I know You do hear prayer
All of these years, I've sent up there

Not my will but Yours be done
That was said by Your Son
I am not as good as He
And that's the way it is with me.

CHORUS:

Lord, I'm just one of Your children
Lord, I'm just one of Your children
I cannot make it by myself
Oh Lord, help me to make it through

Just Trust In Me

Though the trials and tests are heavy to bare,
God is one who really cares.
He will never let you down,
If we keep standing on God's solid ground.

When the devil comes seeking around,
Just keep on standing on God's solid ground,
He will see there is nothing he can do,
And he will soon be leaving you.

You don't have to worry at all,
For God will not let you fall.
He will supply you with the strength you need,
And you can be very sure to succeed.

CHORUS:

Just trust in Me dear children,
Just trust in Me dear children,
Trust in Me, I'll never fail you My child,
So trust in Me dear children.

Keep Me

Keep me with You Father up above,
Keep me secure in Your precious love,
Keep me beside you all of the time,
So I can never be without Thine.

Keep me clean with out and with in,
Keep me so I can see You in the end,
Keep my thoughts the way it pleases You,
So I can be free from the devil too.

Keep me humble and kind to everyone,
Keep me sweet and thankful for Your Son,
Keep me peaceful and have lots of faith,
So I can see my Savior's face.

Lord I love You, I love You so much.
I want to keep with You in touch.
You've been by my side every night and day.
I want to stay in the straight and narrow way.

Leave It With Jesus

When you've done the best you could,
For He knows you have done the best you can,
For He knows every prayer you've sent up there,
And He will answer each and every one.

You have prayed many years my child,
And He is still working for you,
And He saw those tears,
You have shed through the years,
And there will be an answer to each one.

Some children have gone astray,
For He knows how much we have prayed,
For He knows just how to bring them back,
And He will bring those that will come.

CHORUS:

Oh my child, my child, please leave it with Jesus,
Please leave it with Jesus, please leave it with Jesus.
For He knows what to do,
He'll never, no never forsake you.

Let Him Comfort You

Let Him comfort you my child
Let Him comfort you my child
The road may be rough and rocky
Just let Him comfort you my child

There are many things that come our way
As we travel on this journey
But God is right there beside you
So let Him comfort you my child

He'll never fail you my child
In our most hardest trials
He'll be there whispering to you
"Let Me comfort you my child"

CHORUS

Let Him comfort you my child
Let Him comfort you my child
No matter what the problem may be
Let Him comfort you my child

Let It Be

Some of our love ones are not saved.
You know Lord what it takes.
Whatever it takes, Lord,
Let it be Lord, let it be.

There are those who don't live right.
You see them in Your eye sight.
So whatever it takes, Lord,
Let it be Lord, let it be.

Some of Your children have backslid,
And it grieves Your heart, also.
Whatever it takes, Lord,
Let it be Lord, let it be.

CHORUS:

Let it be Lord, let it be.
Whatever it takes, Lord,
Let it be Lord, let it be.

Live For The Lord

Lord, I've done what I could
To the best I can
There's no further that
I can go

I have prayed and I have prayed
To the Father that's above
Who keeps me in His sweet love

I have fasted more than
Once for what we need
You have never failed me at all

If there is more that
You want me to do
Please show me, show me dear Lord

Just tell me dear Lord
And I surely will do it
For you know what I should do
If there is no more you
Want me to do
Then Lord it's all up to you

CHORUS:

Oh Lord I know you will
Answer all prayers
Oh Lord I know you will
Answer all prayers
That I have sent up there

Just live for God down here
Just live for God down here
Obey His word as you live down here

Look

Look what the Lord has done.
He giveth "Jesus Christ's Life", the best,
So we could have salvation and sweet rest.
Oh look what the Lord has done.

Look what the Lord has done.
He gives us our shelter and food.
He giveth transportation and protection too.
Oh look what the Lord has done.

Look what the Lord has done.
He works out our problems that's hard.
He has been by our sides and not afar.
Oh look what the Lord has done.

Look what the Lord has done.
He giveth each breath that we may breathe,
He giveth our eye sight that we may see.
Oh look what the Lord has done.

Look what the Lord has done.
He helps us over the rough seas of life,
And gave us the strength for the devil we fight.
Oh look what the Lord has done.

Love You

My little child I love you so.
I will do everything just give me a call.
Then, you will see just what I can do.
My little child I am waiting for you.

I will not forsake you my little child.
I'm just waiting for you to come,
So don't be afraid I'll not hurt you.
I've helped many people, and I will help you.

Kneel down and pray I will be there,
Because I really love you, and I really care.
You'll soon have the help you needed.
My little child you can count on Me.

My Dear Tawanda

My dear Tawanda you're straying away.
It hurt's our heart I really must say.
We still love you and always will.
You're our own flesh and blood still.
We feel so sorry for you are in sin.
What if God would call you in?
I beg you to follow God up above,
Who really loves you in His sweet love.
I cried and cried so many times,
Praying for you, for you are mine.
Please put God first in your life.
Then your family for that is right,
After that comes whoever you may.
Sorry you chose someone already astray.
Sorry you're in the darkness of the night.
Hope you start seeing the beauty of the light.
I did the best I really could.
Sorry it seems you never understood.
My dear Tawanda I did my best,
And it's up to you to do the rest.
God don't force His self on anyone.
He wants you to willing come.
He's standing there with out stretched hands,
Wanting you to come and hold them tighter than a band.
That's all He can really, really do.
My dear Tawanda we all love you.

My Little Child

Just leave it to Jesus my little child.
He will always come and help you out.
He will always be with you every step of each mile.
Just leave it to Jesus my little child.

When everyone leaves you all alone,
Just pray to Jesus on His big phone.
He will give you the help you needed so long.
Just leave it to Jesus my little child.

When things are getting rough for you to take,
Just lean on the Savior for your sake.
He will be right there with you for His power is great.
Just leave it to Jesus my little child.

CHORUS:

Why not leave it with Jesus my little child?
Why not leave it with Jesus my little child?
He will be there all the time.
So leave it with Jesus, leave it with Jesus my little child.

My Precious Lord

HELP ME LORD, HELP ME LORD NOT
TO FORGET TO PRAY TODAY
HELP ME LORD, HELP ME LORD NOT
TO COMMIT ANY SINS TODAY
HELP ME LORD, HELP ME LORD ALL
OF THE WAY THROUGH

OH MY PRECIOUS LORD, PRECIOUS LORD
KEEP ME IN TOUCH WITH YOU TODAY
PRECIOUS LORD, PRECIOUS LORD
PLEASE KEEP ME SAVED TODAY
PRECIOUS LORD, PRECIOUS LORD TO
SHOW SOMEONE THE WAY

Oh Lord

Oh Lord help people to see,
That they should give their lives to Thee.
You are the best Friend that they have.
Help them Oh Lord that they will see.

Oh Lord help them that's in need,
To simply have faith and in You believe.
You hear the prayers that are said,
And You will give them what they need.

Oh Lord help them that's in test,
To let You have it and simply rest.
There's nothing impossible for You,
When we have did our very best.

Oh My Jesus

Oh my Jesus I love You so,
It's so good that I really know,
A Savior that can help me all the time.
I want to be forever with Thine,
And I love You all the time,
And I love You all the time.

You give me all the help I need,
For everything as I pray on my knees,
You hear my prayer and see the tears,
As I've gone through life all these years,
And I love You all the time,
And I love You all the time.

You've never left me all behind.
You were always there and so kind,
When others were gone You were always there,
You've always treated people right and fair,
And I love You all the time,
And I love You all the time.

Prayer Our Father

Our Father help, help us this day
To stay in the straight and narrow way
Help keep our eyes on the Father up above
And stay secure in His sweet love

Our Father help, help us to stay
True and faithful to each other we pray
Help our love to get deeper than the start
When we are together and be apart

Precious Lord

Stand beside me my precious Lord
    And help me through
Stand beside me my precious Lord
    I really need you
To go through my trials and test
    That come my way
Stand beside me my precious Lord
    All the way through

Be with me my precious Lord
    Through the storms of life
Be with me my precious Lord
    To do what's right
As I go through my darkness hour
Be with me my precious Lord
    All of the way
Help me to love the Father up above
    And obey every word He say

Put It In God's Hand

When you don't know what to do,
And there's nothing you can do,
Just put it in God's hand,
For He knows what you're going through.

The devil maybe all around you,
But remember you and God's ties,
And hold to faith in Jesus Christ.
God will never, never let you down.

Your heart maybe aching in things about life,
Remember what God has promised us.
It will surely help you out,
So keep on walking, walking with Jesus Christ.

CHORUS:

Just put it in the hands of God.
Just put it in the hands of God.
He will take care of everything,
And stop the devil right off.
He have power to make you and me,
And the power over the devil too,
So just put it in God's hand.

Really Need

Jesus is all we need
He sees our every care
As we live on Earth down here
Jesus is all we really need

Things are getting rough down here
In this life it's kinda tough
There are really things we can fear
Jesus is all we really need

CHORUS:

Jesus is all we really need
Jesus is all we really need
He knows just what to do
Jesus is all we really need

Renew Me

Renew my strength,
Renew my hope,
To follow You.
I want to be,
As close as I can,
And follow Thee.
Help me dear Lord,
Very much to always love You.
Renew my strength,
Renew my hope,
To follow You.

Renew my strength,
Renew my hope,
To go through my test.
Help me through my trials,
To hold on to You.
Help me to have faith,
When we have to wait.
Renew my strength,
Renew my hope,
To be patient.

Renew my strength,
Renew my hope,
To resist the devil.
Help me to be very aware,
When he's around.
I know he is very shrewd,
But You are shrewder.
Help me not to be afraid,
Because You have all power.
Renew my strength,
Renew my hope,
To trust in You.

Safely Through

Christ will see you safely through
No matter how dark it looks
He will be right there with you
Christ will help you safely through

Just kneel and say a prayer
You will find Christ waiting there
Ready to give a helping hand
Just Believe it because He can

When things are getting rough
Remember that God is helping you through
He will take care of you
Just Believe it because it's true

See What God Has Done

See what God has done.
He made the earth and sun.
Just believe and be true,
You'll see what He can do.

He can calm all fears
That we may have down here.
And He is always near,
So don't have any fears.

Just ask Him and you'll see,
He will give you all your needs,
And you can see it be
Right before your eyes, you'll see.

He'll answer all your prayers
And help your burdens you bare.
If you'll have faith, He'll be there,
And He does really care.

He has done a lot for me,
And He'll do the same for you.
And I know it you see,
For I've prayed on my knees.

Just ask Him and have faith,
Even if you have to wait,
He knows what it will take.
Lord help me to keep faith.

He will never let you down,
For His word is very sound.
If you stand on God's solid ground
And believe it, He'll stay around.

CHORUS:

See what God has done.
He gave His only Son
Because He loved everyone.
So why not serve Him?
See what He has done,
See what He has done,
See what He has done,
And you will love Him.

Somewhere

Somewhere God is calling you
Somewhere to listen to Him
Somewhere God is wanting you
To give your heart to Him

Somewhere God is seeing you
Somewhere asking for Him
Somewhere God is seeing you
Somewhere seeking for Him

Somewhere God will answer you
Somewhere as you pray
Somewhere you will be rejoicing
Because you gave your heart to Him

Somewhere you will be working
For Him in this life
Someday your life
Will be ending down here on this Earth

You don't have to fear anything
For you are His
You will go to that home up
Above He prepared for us.
And we will be happy with Him
Up above for an eternity

Stand By The Lord

I will stand beside the Lord.
He has stood beside me.
He has never let me down.
He is always around.

Oh how I love my precious Lord.
He has always loved me.
He gives me all I need,
And I know it you see.

I will trust in my Lord.
He will fight my battles you see.
I don't have to be afraid,
For He is looking already ahead.

Sweetly Rest My Soul In Jesus

REST MY SOUL SWEETLY IN JESUS
REST MY SOUL SWEETLY IN JESUS

HE'S THE ONE WHO CAN HELP YOU
HE'S THE ONE WHO CAN HELP YOU

THROUGH THIS WORLD WHERE THERE IS DARKNESS
SWEETLY REST MY SOUL

WE HAVE TO LIVE RIGHT DOWN HERE
WE HAVE TO LIVE RIGHT DOWN HERE

THOUGH THE TRIALS & TESTS ARE HARD
THOUGH THE TRIALS & TESTS ARE HARD

WE WILL HAVE TO SEEK THE LORD
SWEETLY REST MY SOUL

HE'S THE ONE WHO FEEDETH THE SOUL
HE'S THE ONE WHO FEEDETH THE SOUL

HE'S THE ONE WHO KEEPETH THE SOUL
HE'S THE ONE WHO KEEPETH THE SOUL

SO WE WILL GET TO HEAVEN
SWEETLY REST MY SOUL

HE'S THE ONE THAT WE MUST FOLLOW
HE'S THE ONE THAT WE MUST FOLLOW

THAT'S THE WAY WE GET TO HEAVEN
THAT'S THE WAY WE GET TO HEAVEN

THEN WE WILL BE IN GLORY
WE WILL SWEETLY REST

Take Faith

Though many things may seem so dark,
But my Father is waiting there
For you to come and believe in Him.
Take faith and believe in God.

Our trials may seem like a high mountain,
To God it is very simple,
You just have to believe His word
And take faith and believe in God.

We may have a very complex problem.
All it takes is a whisper to God.
He will hear your faintest prayer.
So have faith in God and believe.

CHORUS:

Take faith and believe in God
He will never let you down
The devil may be all around
Please take faith and believe in God

Take The Lord By His Hand

Sometimes we may be in distress,
    Down here.
Sometimes we feel an awful unrest,
    Down here.
But God is watching over you,
So don't forget to watch Him too,
For His hand is right there for you.

There's not much love in this world,
    Down here.
There's not much care in people's hearts,
    Down here.
But keep your eyes on Jesus Christ,
For He gave His only life,
So keep on holding to His hand right there.

People may do you very wrong,
    Down here.
They may plan to treat you wrong,
    Down here.
But God sees them from His throne,
And He will protect His very own,
So keep on holding to His hand right there.

CHORUS:

Take the Lord by His hand
    And leave it there
Take the Lord by His hand
    And leave it there
Don't let the devil discourage you
And make you lose your blessing too
Take the Lord by His hand
    And leave it there.

Thank You Lord

I thank you Lord for giving her to me
And she thanks you for the same, you see
We love each other so very much
Please keep us with you in touch

It took a while but you finally got us together
I thank you and now it's much better
Our love is true and it comes from our heart
Oh Lord help us not to depart

We are starting now in our new life together
Help our lives to get better and better
Help our love to grow deeper and deeper
And God you stay our daily keeper

Thank You Lord For Giving Me A Son

Thank you Lord for giving
    Me a son
Who could help me see
Things clearly
Thank you Lord for a
    Christian son
Who does help me be in this
    Life more cheery

Thank you Lord for blessing
    Me with a Christian Son
One who will do his very best
    To help me one way or another
That can help me go a little further
Thank you for a son
    Who will listen to me
Thank you for
    A son
Who, in his own way, helps me to see
    What I don't understand

This Son is young just 17
    He has trials and test – yes
The devil comes against him – yes
But through God's help and prayer
This son comes out a winner
    He's been living for God since
    A child up and with God's help
    He will reach his goal (eternal life)
To rest the most important thing in life
    His soul

The End Of The Tunnel

THERE'S A LIGHT AT THE END OF THE TUNNEL
THERE'S A LIGHT AT THE END OF THE TUNNEL

IT MAY SEEM KINDA DARK RIGHT NOW
BUT THERE'S LIGHT AT THE END OF THE TUNNEL

THERE'S A LIGHT AT THE END OF THE TUNNEL
THERE'S A LIGHT AT THE END OF THE TUNNEL

THE TRIALS AND TESTS MAY SEEM VERY HARD
BUT THERE'S LIGHT AT THE END OF THE TUNNEL

THERE'S A LIGHT AT THE END OF THE TUNNEL
THERE'S A LIGHT AT THE END OF THE TUNNEL

THOUGH THE SICKNESS AND PAIN ARE HARD TO BEAR
BUT THERE'S A LIGHT AT THE END OF THE TUNNEL

THERE'S A LIGHT AT THE END OF THE TUNNEL
THERE'S A LIGHT AT THE END OF THE TUNNEL

YOU DON'T HAVE TO HAVE NO FEARS
FOR THERE'S LIGHT AT THE END OF THE TUNNEL

There's Nothing

You've done a whole lot for me.
I know it for it is true.
He'll do the same for others if they only believe.
Lord there's nothing You can't do.

You done the things impossible for man,
And it's hard for them to understand.
They are amazed at the things they see You do.
Lord there's nothing You can't do.

Things are here at God's command.
It's all in Genesis you can read.
He made me and you, you can see for yourself,
There is nothing, no nothing He can't do.

CHORUS:

Lord there's nothing You can't do.
Lord there's nothing You can't do.
No there is nothing, no nothing impossible with You.
Lord there's nothing You can't do.

Through This Day

Oh my Jesus help me through this day,
To stay in the heavenly way.
Give me strength from the Father up above,
To stay secure in His wonderful Love.

There are trials and tests we must face,
As we go through this Christian race.
You've been with me through them all,
To try and help me not to fall.

The mountain may seem so hard to climb,
But with God we will make it just fine.
At the end, we will get our reward,
For that's what we've been working for.

Tomorrow

Though our tests may bring us sorrow
And the trials may be very hard,
But through them we always learn
Just what the Savior can do.

We don't know what comes tomorrow,
But our Father will be there
To help us through the pain we bare.
Oh my God, He really cares.

I don't care about tomorrow
For it may not ever come,
I just want to stay with Jesus
And make Heaven my home.

CHORUS:

I don't know about tomorrow
For it's God's and He only knows.
We just have to stay ready
And be ready at God's call.

Travel This Christian Route

The tears may run down my face
    At any place.
The tears may run down my face
    At any place,
But my Father is there, I'm not giving up,
Because my Father will be by my side.

The road maybe rough and rocky
    At any time.
The road maybe rough and rocky
    At any time,
But my mind is made up, I'm not going back,
Because I want to make Heaven my home.

The fiery darts maybe flying
    Thick or thin.
The fiery darts maybe flying
    Thick or thin.
I'm going to be firm, because I love Him,
So I can be with my Savior up there.

CHORUS:

I'm going to travel this Christian route.
I'm going to travel this Christian route.
The devil may come like a flood,
And try to overcome me, but
I'm going to travel this route.

Wedding

There is Bridegroom waiting there,
For the Bride whom is coming with care.
This is a very special time,
For it is a commitment for Thine.
The Father is up above,
Making them one in love,
That they will share from their heart,
Until death do them part.

Help them to love and stay together,
Down through life as they go,
Help them to be watchful and be prayerful,
For the devil will always be right there,
To make them give up in despair.

Now they are together, so please keep them,
The devil will always be somewhere,
So we pray heavenly Father, keep them in Your care,
For You can be there anywhere,
And they are Yours to keep.

CHORUS:

Help their love to grow deeper
                grow deeper
                grow deeper
                grow deeper
So they will have a happy life,
Help them to keep their commitment
                their commitment
                their commitment
                their commitment
For that is so right.

Whatever It Takes Lord I Will Do

There are trials & test
    I face
But I must go through them
    At God's pace
    It kinda looks dreary.
    But Lord help me!
What ever it takes Lord, please help me

The devil is roaring far & near
We only have to face him
    And persevere
It looks so dark Lord
    But please help me
What ever it takes Lord I will do

There are sickness I must face
I must go through them with God's Grace
I gets so weary
But please help me
What ever it takes Lord I will do

Sometimes I feel so all alone
But God sees me from his throne
Please have mercy
    Oh Lord help me
    What ever it takes Lord I will do

Keep me Dear Jesus
    On the right path
I want to see my Savior's face
    He's been so good to me
He has helped me to run
    This Christian race
You know what it takes Lord
    To see your face
What ever it takes Lord I will do

It may take Lord trials & test
    There are things I have to go through
I'm going through trials and test

Man will deceive you
And leave you tattered & torn
You can't trust man

There are relatives and friends
They will do the best they can
You can't trust them fully

The road may be rocky – down here
But I will take the narrow road
Because the wide road will send you
      To Hell
What ever it takes Lord I will do

CHORUS:

What ever it takes Lord
      I will do
Whatever it takes Lord
      I will do
You know what's coming my way you see
What ever it takes Lord I will do

What He Can Do

God's never too late,
In solving your case.
He will be right there beside you,
He'll never let you down.

When the devil is raging around,
Just stand still on God's solid ground.
He will be there every minute, every hour and every day,
Just helping you in every way.

When discouragement comes your way,
Just kneel right down and pray.
He will come to your rescue right away,
And give you the help you need.

CHORUS:

That's what He can do for you,
That's what He can do for you,
He will take your burdens,
And lift you out,
Oh that's what He can do for you.

What's Evers God's Wills

There are sometimes we want our way,
But God sees the future that we cannot see.
And we must be humble and accept God's way.
What's evers Your wills Lord let it be.

The load may be heavy, so heavy to bare,
But You are looking and You really care.
He will help us to carry the load that we bare.
What's evers Your wills Lord let it be.

Sometimes it's hard to know God's wills,
But God will come and let you know His will.
Then we will know just what to do.
What's evers Your wills Lord let it be.

CHORUS:

What's evers Your wills Lord
    Let it be,
What's evers Your wills Lord
    Let it be.
You know what's best Lord
    For us You see.
What's evers Your wills Lord
    Please let it be.

When It Seems No One Cares

When trials and tests come your way,
    Jesus cares
And it makes you have a dreary day,
    Jesus cares
When you've done your very best,
Don't give up, let Jesus do the rest
For the Lord is always there
    And Jesus cares

When you are down and low in spirit,
    Jesus cares
When it seems you can't bare it,
    Jesus cares
When you've gone as far as you can,
Don't give up, but hold to God's hand,
For the Lord is always there
    And Jesus cares

When discouragement comes your way,
    Jesus cares
When it seems you can't think of what to pray,
    Jesus cares
When the devil is raging all around,
Just stand firm on God's solid ground,
For the Lord is always there
    And Jesus cares

CHORUS:

When it seems no one cares,
    Jesus does
When it seems no one has love to share,
    Jesus does
When it seems people let you down,
Don't give up and lose your Crown,
For the Lord is always there
    And Jesus cares

Wherever We Are, Trust In God

Over the sea
God is with you and me
Wherever we will be
He will give us what we need
So don't worry He'll take care of you and me

High in the sky
He is preparing for you and I
A beautiful home that you can't see with the eye
But be thankful He loves you and I

For those trials and tests
Let God have them and rest
He's got the power and He'll do what is best
You can count on God just lean on His breast

Wherever You Are

Wherever You are Lord,
I want to be.
Wherever You are Lord,
I want to be.
Through the stormy, stormy sea,
Wherever You are Lord,
I want to be.

Wherever You are Lord,
I want to be.
Wherever You are Lord,
I want to be.
Through the dark shadows, I want to see.
Wherever You are Lord,
I want to be.

Wherever You are Lord,
I want to be.
Wherever You are Lord,
I want to be.
Through the trials and tests, I see.
Wherever You are Lord,
I want to be.

Wherever You are Lord,
I want to be.
Wherever You are Lord,
I want to be.
No matter what happens to me.
Wherever You are Lord,
I want to be.

Will Stand

I will stand, will stand by Christ,
For He gave His only life,
For you and for me He shed His blood,
I will stand, will stand by Christ.

I will live, will live for Christ,
For that's the right way to go,
So we could go, could go to heaven and be
With Him, with Him up above.

I will love, will love Jesus Christ,
For He'll do all things for you,
For He'll do, He'll do what you ask Him to do.
He'll never, no never forsake you.

He's my friend, my best friend I have,
And He will be until the end.
He will be, for me a friend I didn't know,
And now, and now I know.

Yes, Dear Lord

Yes dear Lord I love You so.
I want You to really know.
So many people pay You no mind,
After You've been so very kind.

    Oh dear Lord You are so wonderful.
    I am going to stay with Thee.

You've taught me so very much.
Keep Your hand for me to touch.
I want to be just as close as I can,
And hold to Your hand as tight as a band.

    Oh dear Lord You are so wonderful.
    I am going to stay with Thee.

It's so good to really know You,
And all of Your privileges too.
It's so good not to be bound,
By the devil that's all around.

    Oh dear Lord You are so wonderful.
    I am going to stay with Thee.

www.ingramcontent.com/pod-product-compliance
Lightning Source LLC
Chambersburg PA
CBHW071711090426
42738CB00009B/1740